Silo's Message

Silo's Message

The Book
The Experience
The Path

Latitude Press

Note from the Printers

The Message given by Silo in July of 2002 consists of three parts: The Book, The Experience, and the Path.

The Book has been known for some time under the title *The Inner Look*.

The Experience is expressed through eight ceremonies.

The Path is a collection of reflections and suggestions.

This edition contains the Message in its entirety. Circulating in both printed and electronic form, it is being made freely available to those who wish to use it.

CONTENTS

THE BOOK

The Inner Look   1

THE EXPERIENCE

THE PATH

THE BOOK

The Inner Look

I. MEDITATION

1. Here it tells how the non-meaning of life can be converted into meaning and fulfillment.
2. Here are joy, love of the body, of nature, of humanity, and of the spirit.
3. Here sacrifices, feelings of guilt, and threats from the beyond are rejected.
4. Here the worldly is not opposed to the eternal.
5. Here it tells of the inner revelation at which all arrive who carefully meditate in humble search.

II. DISPOSITION TO COMPREHEND

1. I know how you feel because I can experience your state, but you do not know how to experience the things I am speaking of. Therefore, if I speak to you without self-interest of that which makes the human being happy and free, it is worth your while to try to comprehend.

2. Do not think that you will arrive at understanding by arguing with me. You may do so if you believe that in this way your understanding will become clearer, but it is not the appropriate path in this case.

3. If you ask me what attitude is appropriate, I will tell you that it is to meditate profoundly and without haste on what is explained here.

4. If you reply that you are busy with more urgent things, I will answer that since your wish is to sleep or to die, I will do nothing to oppose it.

5. Nor should you argue that you dislike my way of presenting things, for you do not criticize the peel when you like the fruit.
6. I state things in the way I consider appropriate, not as might be desired by those who aspire to things remote from inner truth.

III. NON-MEANING

Over many days I discovered this great paradox: Those who bore failure in their hearts were able to illuminate the final victory, while those who felt triumphant were left by the wayside, vegetating in their muted and diffuse life. Over many days, coming from the darkest of darkness, I arrived at the light, guided not by teachings but by meditation.

Thus, I told myself on the first day:

1. There is no meaning in life if everything ends with death.
2. All justification for actions, whether these actions are despicable or admirable, is always a new dream that leaves only emptiness ahead.
3. God is something uncertain.
4. Faith is something as variable as reason and dreams.

5. "What one should do" may be thoroughly discussed, but in the end there is nothing that definitively supports any position.

6. The "responsibility" of those who commit themselves to something is no greater than the responsibility of those who do not.

7. I move according to my interests, and this makes me neither a coward nor a hero.

8. "My interests" neither justify nor discredit anything.

9. "My reasons" are no better than the reasons of others, nor are they worse.

10. Cruelty horrifies me, but neither because of this nor in itself is it better or worse than kindness.

11. What I or others say today is of no value tomorrow.

12. To die is not better than to live or never to have been born, but neither is it worse.

13. I discovered, not through teachings, but through experience and meditation, that there is no meaning in life if everything ends with death.

IV. DEPENDENCE

The second day.

1. Nothing that I do, feel, or think depends on
   me.
2. I am mutable and depend on the action of my
   surroundings. When I want to change my
   environment or my "I," it is the environment
   that ends up changing me. Then I seek the
   city or nature, social redemption or a new
   struggle that will justify my existence. In
   every case it is my environment that leads me
   to choose one attitude or another. In this way,
   my interests and my surroundings leave me
   here.
3. I say, then, that it does not matter who or
   what decides. I say on these occasions that I
   have to live since I am in the situation of
   living. I say all this, but there is nothing that
   justifies it. I can make a decision, hesitate, or
   remain where I am. In any case, one thing is

only provisionally better than another; ultimately there is no better or worse.

4. If someone tells me that those who do not eat die, I will answer that this is indeed so, and that, spurred by their needs, they are compelled to eat. But I will not add that the struggle to eat justifies one's existence—nor will I say that this struggle is bad. I will simply say that all of this concerns an individual or collective fact related to the need for subsistence, but that it has no meaning in the moment that the last battle is lost.

5. I will say, moreover, that I feel solidarity with the struggle of the poor, the exploited, and the persecuted. I will say that I feel "fulfilled" in this identification, but I understand that these feelings do not justify anything.

V. INTIMATION OF MEANING

The third day.

1. At times I have anticipated events that later took place.
2. At times I have grasped a distant thought.
3. At times I have described places I have never been.
4. At times I have recounted exactly what took place in my absence.
5. At times an immense joy has surprised me.
6. At times a total comprehension has overwhelmed me.
7. At times a perfect communion with everything has filled me with ecstasy.
8. At times I have broken through my reveries and seen reality in a new way.
9. At times I have seen something for the first time, yet recognized it as though I had seen it before.

…And all this has made me think. It is clear to me that without these experiences I could not have emerged from the non-meaning.

VI. SLEEP AND AWAKENING

The fourth day.

1. I cannot take as real what I see in my dreams, nor what I see in semi-sleep, nor what I see when I am awake but in reverie.

2. I can take as real what I see when I am awake and without reveries. Here I am not speaking of what my senses register, since naive and dubious "data" can arrive from my external and internal senses as well as from my memory. Rather, I am speaking of the activities of my mind as they relate to the "data" being thought. What is valid is that when my mind is awake it "knows" and when it is asleep it "believes." Only rarely do I perceive reality in a new way, and it is then that I realize that what I normally see resembles sleep or semi-sleep.

There is a real way of being awake, and it has led me to meditate profoundly on all that has been said so far. It has, moreover, opened the door for me to discover the meaning of all that exists.

VII. PRESENCE OF THE FORCE

The fifth day.

1. When I was truly awake I scaled from comprehension to comprehension.

2. When I was truly awake yet lacked the strength to continue the ascent, I was able to draw the Force from within myself. This Force was present throughout my body. All of the energy was present even in the smallest cells of my body, and it circulated more rapidly and more intensely than my blood.

3. I discovered that the energy concentrated in those points of my body that were active, and was absent when they were not.

4. During illness the energy was either lacking or it accumulated precisely in the areas of my body that were affected. But if I was able to reestablish the normal flow of the energy, many illnesses began to recede.

Some peoples knew this, and through various procedures that seem strange to us today they were able to reestablish the flow of the energy.

Some peoples knew this, and they were able to communicate this energy to others, producing "illuminations" of comprehension and even physical "miracles."

VIII. CONTROL OF THE FORCE

The sixth day.

1. There is a way of directing and concentrating the Force that circulates through the body.
2. In the body are points of control on which depend what we know as movement, emotion, and idea. When the energy acts in these points it gives rise to motor, emotional, and intellectual manifestations.
3. Depending on whether the energy acts more internally or superficially in the body, the states of deep sleep, semi-sleep, or wakefulness arise. Surely, the halos that surround the bodies or heads of the saints (or the great awakened ones) in religious paintings allude to this phenomenon of the energy, which on occasion manifests more externally.

4. There is a point of control of being-truly-awake, and there is a way of bringing the Force to this point.
5. When the energy is led to this point, all the other points of control move in a new way.

Upon understanding this and hurling the Force to this superior point, my entire body felt the impact of an enormous energy. This energy struck powerfully within my consciousness, and I ascended from comprehension to comprehension. But I also observed that if I lost control of the energy I could descend to the depths of the mind. Then, seeing the dividing line between these mental states, I remembered the legends of "heavens" and "hells."

IX. MANIFESTATIONS OF THE ENERGY

The seventh day.

1. This energy in motion could become "independent" of the body yet still maintain its unity.

2. This unified energy was really a sort of "double" of the body, corresponding to the coenesthetic representation of one's own body within the space of representation. The sciences that deal with mental phenomena have not paid sufficient attention to the existence of this space or to the representations that correspond to the internal sensations of the body.

3. The energy duplicated in this way, that is, imagined as if "outside" the body or "separated" from its material base, either dissolved as an image or was represented correctly, depending on the internal unity of the one carrying out this work.

4. I was able to confirm that the "exterioriza-tion" of this energy, which represented one's body as "outside" of one's body, could be produced even from the lowest levels of the mind. In these cases, a threat to the most basic unity of the living being provoked this response in order to safeguard the one who was in danger. That is why, in the trances of some mediums whose level of consciousness was low and whose internal unity was imper-iled, these responses occurred involuntarily and were not recognized as being self-pro-duced, but were attributed to other entities.

The "ghosts" of certain peoples, like the "spirits" of some fortune-tellers, were nothing but the "doubles" (the self-representations) of those who felt themselves possessed. Having lost control of the Force, their mental state was darkened in trance, and they felt controlled by strange beings that at times produced remark-able phenomena. Doubtless this was the case of many who were said to be "possessed." What was decisive, then, was control of the Force.

All this changed completely my conception of both daily life and of life after death. Through these thoughts and experiences I began to lose faith in death, and now I no longer believe in it, just as I no longer believe in the non-meaning of life.

X. EVIDENCE OF MEANING

The eighth day.

1. The real importance of an awakened life became evident to me.
2. The real importance of eliminating internal contradictions convinced me.
3. The real importance of mastering the Force in order to achieve unity and continuity filled me with joyful meaning.

XI. THE LUMINOUS CENTER

The ninth day.

1. In the Force was "the light" that came from a "center."
2. In withdrawal from the center there was a dissolution of the energy, while in the unification and evolution of the energy that luminous center was at work.

It did not strike me as strange to find a devotion to the Sun-god among ancient peoples. And I understood that while some worshipped this heavenly object because it gave life to the earth and to nature, others recognized in that majestic body the symbol of a greater reality.

There were those who went still further and received innumerable gifts from this center, gifts that at times "descended" as tongues of fire over the inspired ones, at times arrived as luminous spheres, and at times appeared as burning bushes before the fearful believer.

XII. THE DISCOVERIES

The tenth day.

Few but important were my discoveries, which I summarize this way:

1. Though the Force circulates through the body involuntarily, it can be directed through conscious effort. Achieving an intentional change in the level of consciousness grants the human being an important glimpse of liberation from the "natural" conditions that seem to impose themselves on the consciousness.
2. Within the body are points that control its diverse activities.
3. There are differences between the state of being-truly-awake and other levels of consciousness.
4. The Force can be led to the point of real awakening (understanding by "Force" the mental energy that accompanies particular

images and by "point" the location of such an image in a certain "place" in the space of representation).

These conclusions led me to recognize in the prayers of ancient peoples the seed of a great truth—a truth later obscured by external rites and practices, making it impossible for them to develop that internal work which, realized with perfection, puts human beings in contact with their luminous source. Finally, I observed that my "discoveries" were not discoveries at all, but arose from the inner revelation at which all arrive who, without contradictions, search for the light in their own hearts.

XIII. THE PRINCIPLES

Different is the attitude toward life and things when inner revelation strikes like lightning.

Following the steps slowly, meditating on what has been said and what has yet to be said, you may convert the non-meaning into meaning. It is not indifferent what you do with your life. Your life, subject to laws, is open to possibilities among which you can choose. I do not speak to you of liberty. I speak to you of liberation, of movement, of process. I do not speak to you of liberty as something static, but of liberating yourself step-by-step, as those who approach their city become liberated from the road already traveled. Thus, "what one must do" depends not upon distant, incomprehensible, and conventional morals, but upon laws: laws of life, of light, of evolution.

Here are the "Principles" which can help you in your search for internal unity:

THE PRINCIPLES

1. To go against the evolution of things is to go against yourself.
2. When you force something toward an end, you produce the contrary.
3. Do not oppose a great force. Retreat until it weakens, then advance with resolution.
4. Things are well when they move together, not in isolation.
5. If day and night, summer and winter are well with you, you have surpassed the contradictions.
6. If you pursue pleasure, you enchain yourself to suffering. But as long as you do not harm your health, enjoy without inhibition when the opportunity presents itself.
7. If you pursue an end, you enchain yourself. If everything you do is realized as though it were an end in itself, you liberate yourself.
8. You will make your conflicts disappear when you understand them in their ultimate root, not when you want to resolve them.
9. When you harm others you remain enchained, but if you do not harm anyone you can freely do whatever you want.

10. When you treat others as you want them to treat you, you liberate yourself.
11. It does not matter in which faction events have placed you. What matters is that you comprehend that you have not chosen any faction.
12. Contradictory or unifying actions accumulate within you. If you repeat your acts of internal unity, nothing can detain you.

You will be like a force of Nature when it finds no resistance in its path. Learn to distinguish a difficulty, a problem, an obstacle, from a contradiction. While those may move you or spur you on, contradiction traps you in a closed circle with no way out.

Whenever you find great strength, joy, and kindness in your heart, or when you feel free and without contradictions, immediately be internally thankful. When you find yourself in opposite circumstances, ask with faith, and the gratitude you have accumulated will return to you transformed and amplified in benefit.

XIV. GUIDE TO THE INNER ROAD

If you understand what I have explained so far, you can, through a simple exercise, readily experience the manifestation of the Force. It is not the same, however, to search for the correct mental position (as if this were a question of approaching a technical task) as it is to enter the kind of emotional tone and openness that poetry inspires. The language used to transmit these truths, then, is intended to facilitate an attitude that makes it easier to be in the presence of internal perception, rather than in the presence of an idea of "internal perception."

Now follow attentively what I will explain to you, because it concerns the inner landscape you may encounter when working with the Force, and the directions you can imprint on your mental movements.

"On the inner road you may walk darkened or luminous. Attend to the two roads that open before you.

If you let your being cast itself toward dark regions, your body wins the battle and it dominates. Then, sensations and appearances of spirits, of forces, of memories will arise. On this road you descend further and further. Here dwell Hatred, Vengeance, Strangeness, Possession, Jealousy, and the Desire to Remain. Should you descend even further you will be invaded by Frustration, Resentment, and all those dreams and desires that have brought ruin and death upon humanity.

If you impel your being in a luminous direction, you will find resistance and fatigue at every step. There are things to blame for this fatigue in the ascent. Your life weighs; your memories weigh; your previous actions impede the ascent. The climb is made difficult by the action of your body, which tends to dominate.

In the steps of the ascent you will find strange regions of pure colors and unknown sounds.

Do not flee purification, which acts like fire and horrifies with its phantoms.

Reject startling fears and disheartenment.

Reject the desire to flee toward low and dark regions.

Reject the attachment to memories.

Remain in internal liberty, indifferent toward the dream of the landscape, with resolution in the ascent.

The pure light dawns in the summits of the great mountain chains, and the waters-of-a-thousand-colors flow amid unrecognizable melodies toward crystalline plateaus and prairies.

Do not fear the pressure of the light, which pushes against you with increasing strength the closer you draw to its center. Absorb it as though it were a liquid or a wind—certainly, in it is life.

When you find the hidden city in the great mountain chain you must know the entrance— and you will know it in the moment your life is transformed. Its enormous walls are written in figures, are written in colors, are "sensed." In this city are kept the done and the yet-to-be-done. But for your inner eye the transparent is opaque. Yes, the walls are impenetrable for you!

Take the Force of the hidden city. Return to the world of dense life with your brow and your hands luminous."

XV. THE EXPERIENCE OF PEACE AND THE PASSAGE OF THE FORCE

1. Completely relax your body and quiet your mind. Then, imagine a transparent and luminous sphere that descends toward you until it comes to rest in your heart. In that moment you will recognize that the sphere ceases to appear as an image and transforms into a sensation within your chest.

2. Observe how the sensation of the sphere slowly expands from your heart toward the outside of your body, while your breathing becomes fuller and deeper. When the sensation reaches the limits of your body you may stop there and register the experience of internal peace. You may remain there as long as you feel is appropriate. To conclude the exercise, calm and renewed, reverse the previous expansion, until arriving, as in the beginning, at your heart, and finally releasing the sphere. This work is called the experience of peace.

3. Should you instead wish to experience the passage of the Force, you must increase the expansion rather than reversing it, allowing your emotions and your whole being to follow along. Do not try to pay attention to your breathing; let it act by itself while you follow the expansion outward from your body.

4. Let me repeat: Your attention at such moments must be on the sensation of the expanding sphere. If you are unable to achieve this, it is advisable that you stop and try again another time. In any case, even if you do not produce the passage of the Force you will be able to experience an interesting sensation of peace.

5. If, however, you go further, you will begin to experience the passage of the Force. The sensations from your hands and other areas of your body will have a different tone than usual. Later you may notice increasing undulations, and in a short while vivid images and powerful emotions may arise. Allow the passage to take place...

6. Upon receiving the Force, you will, depending upon your habitual mode of representation, perceive the light or strange sounds. In any case, what is important is that you experience an amplification of consciousness, among whose indicators are a greater lucidity and a disposition to understand what is taking place.

7. If this singular state has not faded with the passage of time, you can bring it to an end whenever you wish by imagining or feeling that the sphere contracts and then leaves you in the same way it arrived in the beginning.

8. It is interesting to recognize that many altered states of consciousness have been and almost always are achieved through the use of mechanisms similar to those described. These may be disguised, however, by strange rituals, or at times reinforced by practices involving extreme fatigue, unbridled motor activity, repetition, and postures that alter the breathing and distort the general sensation of the intrabody. In this domain you should also recognize hypnosis, mediumistic activity, and

the effects of drugs—all of which, though they act through a different pathway, produce similar alterations. Characteristic of all these cases is an absence of control and a lack of awareness of what is taking place. Do not trust such manifestations, and consider them nothing more than "trances" such as those through which dabblers, the ignorant, and (according to legend) even the "saints" have passed.

9. Even if you have followed these recommendations, you may still have been unable to produce the passage of the Force. This should not become a source of concern, however. Simply take it as an indicator of a lack of internal "letting go" which may reflect excessive tensions or problems with the dynamics of the images—in sum, a fragmentation of emotional behavior—something that will, moreover, also be present in your daily life.

XVI. PROJECTION OF THE FORCE

1. If you have experienced the passage of the Force, you will be able to understand how, based on similar experiences but without understanding, various peoples went on to develop rites and cults that later multiplied endlessly. Through experiences like those previously described there were some who felt that their bodies had "doubled," and the experience of the Force gave them the sensation that they could project this energy outside themselves.

2. The Force could be "projected" to others and also to objects particularly "suited" to receive and conserve it. I trust it will not be difficult for you to understand the function filled by the sacraments of various religions, as well as the significance of those sacred places and priests supposedly "charged" with the Force. When certain objects were surrounded with ceremonies and rites and worshipped with

faith in temples, surely they "gave back" to the believers the energy accumulated through repeated prayer. Since fundamental internal experience is essential to understanding in these matters, attempts at understanding based, as is normally the case, solely on externals—whether cultural, geographical, historical, or traditional—reveal a limitation in our knowledge of human realities.

3. "Projecting," "charging," and "replenishing" the Force are subjects to which we will return later. For now let me say that this same mechanism continues to operate even in desacralized societies, where leaders and others imbued with prestige are surrounded by a special aura in the eyes of those who would like to see them, "touch" them, acquire a scrap of their clothing, or their possessions.

4. This occurs because all representations of the "heights" extend from eye level upward, above the normal line of sight. And the "higher-ups" are those who "possess" kindness, wisdom, and strength. There, in the "heights" above, we also find the hierarchies, the powers that be, and the flags of State.

And we, ordinary mortals, must at all costs "ascend" the social ladder in order to draw closer to power. What a sorry state we are in, still governed by these mechanisms that coincide with our internal representation, in which our heads are in the "heights" and our feet stuck on the ground. What an unhappy state we are in, when we believe in these things, and believe in them because they have their own "reality" in our internal representation. What a sorry state we are in, when our external look is nothing but an unacknowledged projection of the internal.

XVII. LOSS AND REPRESSION OF THE FORCE

1. The greatest discharges of energy occur through uncontrolled acts, including unbridled imagination, unchecked curiosity, immoderate small talk, excessive sexuality, and exaggerated perception—looking, listening, tasting, and so on in an aimless and excessive manner. But you should also recognize that many act in these ways because it allows them to discharge tensions that would otherwise be painful. All things considered, and given the function served by these discharges, I am sure you will agree with me that it is not reasonable to repress them but rather to give order to them.

2. As for sexuality, you must interpret this correctly: This function must not be repressed because that will only cause torment and internal contradiction. Sexuality directs itself toward and concludes in the act itself, and it is not useful that it continues affecting the

imagination, or is expressed as an obsessive search for a new object of possession.

3. The control of sex by a particular social or religious "morality" has served purposes that had nothing to do with evolution, but the contrary.

4. In repressed societies, the Force (the energy of the representation of the sensation of the intrabody) turned back toward the crepuscular. In those societies, cases increased of the "possessed," of "witches," of the sacrilegious, and of criminals of all kinds who rejoiced in suffering and the destruction of life and beauty. In some tribes and civilizations the criminals were to be found among both the accusers and the accused. In other cases all that was science and progress was persecuted because it opposed the irrational, the crepuscular, and the repressed.

5. The repression of sex still exists among certain so-called "primitive peoples," just as it does in other so-called "advanced civilizations." It is evident that although the origins of these two situations may differ, both are marked by great destructiveness.

6. If you ask me to explain further, I will tell you that in reality sex is sacred, and it is the center from which all life and creativity springs, just as it is from there that all destruction arises when issues about its functioning are not resolved.

7. Never believe the lies of the poisoners of life when they refer to sex as despicable. On the contrary, in it is beauty, and not in vain is it related to the best feelings of love.

8. Be careful, then, and consider sex a great wonder, which must be treated with care, without turning it into a source of contradiction or disintegration of vital energy.

XVIII. ACTION AND REACTION OF THE FORCE

Earlier I explained to you: "Whenever you find great strength, joy, and kindness in your heart, or when you feel free and without contradictions, immediately be internally thankful."

1. "To be thankful" means to concentrate these positive moods and to associate them with an image, with a representation. If you have previously linked positive states in this way, you can, upon finding yourself in a difficult situation, evoke that representation, and along with it will arise the positive quality that accompanied it earlier. Furthermore, since this mental "charge" has been increased through previous repetitions, it is capable of displacing the negative emotions that certain situations can impose.

2. Thus, whatever you ask for will return from within you amplified in benefit as long as you have accumulated within yourself numerous

positive states. By now it should be unnecessary to repeat that, believing they would respond to prayers and supplication, this mechanism has long been used (though in confused ways) to "charge" external objects or persons, as well as internal entities that have been "projected."

XIX. THE INTERNAL STATES

You must now gain sufficient insight into the various internal states you may find yourself in throughout the course of your life, and particularly in the course of your evolutionary work. I have no way to describe these states except by using images, in this case allegorical ones. These seem to me to have the virtue of "visually" concentrating complex states and moods. The unusual approach of linking these states to one another as if they were distinct moments in a single process introduces a departure from the typically fragmented descriptions to which we have become accustomed from those who normally deal with such things.

1. As I mentioned earlier, in the first state, known as Diffuse Vitality, non-meaning prevails. Here, everything is oriented by physical needs, though these are often confused with contradictory images and desires. Here, both motives and all that is done are shrouded in

darkness. In this state you simply vegetate, lost among changing forms. From this point you can evolve only by following one of two paths: the way of Death or the way of Mutation.

2. The path of Death puts you in the presence of a dark and chaotic landscape. The ancients knew this passage and almost always located it "underground" or in the abysmal depths. There are those who visited this kingdom, to later "resurrect" in luminous levels. Understand well that "below" Death lies Diffuse Vitality. Perhaps the human mind relates mortal disintegration to subsequent phenomena of transformation; perhaps it associates this diffuse movement with what takes place before birth. If your direction is that of ascent, "Death" signifies a break with your former stage. By taking the path of Death you ascend to another state.

3. Arriving here you find yourself at the refuge of Regression. Two ways open from here: One is the road of Repentance; the other, which you used for the ascent, is the road of Death. If you take the first road it is because

your decision tends to break with your past life. If you go back along the road of Death you fall again into the depths, with the sensation of being trapped in a closed circle.

4. Earlier I told you that there is another path you might take to escape from the abyss of Vitality; it is the path of Mutation. If you choose this road it is because you wish to emerge from your unhappy state, but are unwilling to abandon some of its apparent benefits. It is, then, a false road known as the "Twisted Hand." Many are the monsters who have emerged from the depths through this tortuous passageway. They have wanted to storm the heavens without abandoning the hells, and consequently have projected infinite contradiction into the middle world.

5. Let us suppose that by ascending from the kingdom of Death and through your conscious Repentance you have now reached the dwelling of Tendency. Two narrow supports, Conservation and Frustration, sustain your dwelling. Conservation is false and unstable; walking along this path you delude yourself with the idea of permanence, but in reality

you descend rapidly. Should you take the path of Frustration your ascent is arduous, but this path is the only-one-not-false.

6. After failure upon failure you can reach the next resting place, called the "dwelling of deviation." Take care in choosing between the two roads now before you. Either you take the road of Resolution, which carries you to Generation, or you take that of Resentment, which causes you to descend once more toward Regression. Here you face another dilemma: Either you choose the labyrinth of conscious life—and you do so with Resolution—or you return, resentfully, to your previous life. There are many who, at this point, unable to surpass themselves, cut off their own possibilities.

7. But you who have ascended with Resolution now find yourself at the dwelling known as Generation. Here you face three doors: one called the Fall, another known as Intent, and the third called Degradation. The Fall carries you directly to the depths, and only an external accident can push you toward it; it is unlikely that you would choose that door. The door of Degradation, however, carries

you indirectly to the abyss as you retrace your steps in a sort of turbulent spiral in which you continually reconsider all that you have lost and all that you have sacrificed. This examination of consciousness that leads you to Degradation is surely a false examination in which you underestimate and disproportionately evaluate some of what you are comparing. You compare the effort of the ascent with those "benefits" you have left behind. But if you examine things more closely, you will see that you have not abandoned anything for the ascent, but rather for other reasons. Degradation begins, then, when you misrepresent motives that were not really related to the ascent. I ask you now: What betrays the mind? Perhaps it is the false motives of initial enthusiasm? Perhaps it is the difficulty of the undertaking? Perhaps it is the false memories of sacrifices that never were, or that were made for other reasons? Saying this I ask you now: Some time ago your house burned down, and because it did you chose the ascent. Or do you now think that because of this ascent, your house burned down? Have you perhaps noticed what has happened to the other houses around you? There is no doubt that you must choose the middle door, that of Intent.

8. Climbing the stairway of Intent you will reach an unstable dome. From there, take the narrow, winding passageway known as Volubility until you reach a vast and empty space like a platform, which bears the name Open-Space-of-the-Energy.

9. In that open space you may be frightened by the immense, deserted landscape and the ter-rifying silence of this night, transfigured by enormous and immobile stars. There, directly over your head, you will see set in the firma-ment the suggestive form of the Black Moon, a strange, eclipsed moon located exactly opposite the Sun. Here you must await the dawn patiently and with faith, for nothing bad can happen if you remain calm.

10. You may, upon finding yourself in this situa-tion, want to arrange an immediate way out of there. However, should you try to leave instead of prudently awaiting the day, you could end up blindly groping your way anywhere. Remember that all movement here (in the darkness) is false and is generically

called Improvisation. If, forgetting what I tell you now, you begin to improvise movements, be certain that you will be dragged by a whirlwind down paths and past dwellings to the darkest depths of Dissolution.

11. How difficult it is to comprehend that the internal states are linked one to another! If you could see what inflexible logic the consciousness has, you would realize that those who blindly improvise in this situation inevitably begin to degrade themselves and others. Then, feelings of Frustration arise in them, and later they fall into Resentment and finally into Death—forgetting all that they had at one moment managed to perceive.

12. If in that open space you manage to reach the day, the radiant Sun will rise before your eyes, illuminating reality for the first time. Then you will see that in everything that exists there lives a Plan.

13. It is unlikely that you will fall from here unless you should voluntarily choose to descend to obscure regions in order to carry the light into the darkness.

It would not be useful to develop these subjects further, because without experience they can only mislead by transferring to the field of the imaginary something that can actually be achieved. May what has been said here be of service to you. And if you do not find what has been explained here useful, to what could you object, since for skepticism nothing has any basis or reason—it is like the image in a mirror, the sound of an echo, the shadow of a shadow.

XX. INTERNAL REALITY

1. Take note of my considerations. In them you will not only intuit allegorical phenomena and landscapes of the external world, but you will also find true descriptions of the mental world.

2. Nor should you believe that the "places" through which you pass in your journey have some sort of independent existence. Such confusion has often obscured profound teachings, and even today there are some who believe that the heavens, hells, angels, devils, monsters, enchanted castles, distant cities, and the rest have visible reality for the "enlightened." The same prejudice, but with the opposite interpretation, has been maintained by skeptics without wisdom who take these things to be simply "illusions" or "hallucinations" suffered by feverish minds.

3. I must repeat, then: You should understand that all this deals with real mental states,

even though they are symbolized here by objects that correspond to the external world.

4. Remember what I have said, and learn to discover the truth behind the allegories, which on occasion lead the mind astray, but at other times translate realities that would be impossible to grasp without such representation.

When they spoke of a city of the gods, which the heroes of many peoples strove to reach; when they spoke of a paradise where gods and humankind lived together in transfigured original nature; when they spoke of falls and floods, great internal truth was told.

Later, the redeemers brought their messages and came to us in double nature to reestablish that lost unity for which we yearned. Then, too, great inner truth was told.

But when all this was spoken of but set outside the mind it was an error or a lie.

However, the fusing of the inner look with the external world forces this look to travel new paths.

The heroes of this age fly toward the stars.
They fly through regions previously unknown.
They fly out from their world and, without
knowing it, they are impelled toward the inter-
nal and luminous center.

THE EXPERIENCE

Ceremonies

SERVICE

This ceremony is carried out at the request of a group of people.

Officiant: My mind is restless.

Participants: My mind is restless.

Officiant: My heart is troubled.

Participants: My heart is troubled.

Officiant: My body is tense.

Participants: My body is tense.

Officiant: I relax my body, my heart, and my mind.

Participants: I relax my body, my heart, and my mind.

When possible the participants are seated. The Assistant stands, reads a Principle or a passage from The Inner Look *suited to the circumstances, and invites the participants to meditate on it. After a few minutes the Officiant stands and slowly reads the following phrases, pausing after each one.*

Officiant: Completely relax your body and quiet your mind...

Then imagine a transparent and luminous sphere that descends toward you until it comes to rest in your heart...

Notice that the sphere begins to transform into an expanding sensation within your chest...

The sensation of the sphere expands from your heart toward the outside of your body, at the same time that you deepen your breathing...

You will feel new sensations in your hands and the rest of your body…

You will perceive increasing undulations. Positive emotions and memories will arise…

Allow the passage of the Force to take place freely. This Force gives energy to your body and your mind…

Let the Force manifest within you...

Try to see its light within your eyes, and do not stop it from acting by itself…

Feel the Force and its inner light.

Let it manifest freely…

Assistant: With this Force that we have received, let us concentrate our minds on the fulfillment of what we truly need...

The Assistant invites everyone to stand and carry out the Asking. After allowing some time to pass:

Officiant: Peace, Force, and Joy!

Participants: For you also, Peace, Force, and Joy.

LAYING ON OF HANDS

This ceremony is carried out at the request of one or more persons. The Officiant and the Assistant are standing.

Officiant: My mind is restless.

Participants: My mind is restless.

Officiant: My heart is troubled.

Participants: My heart is troubled.

Officiant: My body is tense.

Participants: My body is tense.

Officiant: I relax my body, my heart, and my mind.

Participants: I relax my body, my heart, and my mind.

The Officiant and the Assistant sit down and allow some time to pass. The Officiant stands.

Officiant: If you wish to receive the Force, you should understand that at the moment of the Laying on of Hands you will begin to experience new sensations. You will perceive increasing undulations. Positive emotions and memories will arise. When this occurs, allow the passage of the Force to take place freely...

Let the Force manifest within you, and do not stop it from acting by itself...

Feel the Force and its inner light…

Let the Force manifest freely…

After some time the Assistant stands.

Assistant: Those who wish to receive the Force may stand.

For a large number of participants, the Assistant invites them to remain standing at their seats; for smaller numbers, participants are invited to form a circle around the Officiant. After a brief time the Officiant begins the Laying on of Hands. If necessary, the Assistant may aid the circulation of the participants, at times accompanying some to their seats. Following the Laying on of Hands, some time is given for participants to assimilate the experience.

Assistant: With this Force that we have received, let us concentrate our minds on the fulfillment of what we truly need. Or let us concentrate our minds on the fulfillment of what a loved one truly needs.

The Assistant invites participants to stand and silently carry out their Askings. On occasion one of the participants may formulate an Asking for someone else, whether present or not.

After letting some time pass.

Officiant: Peace, Force, and Joy!

Participants: For you also, Peace, Force, and Joy.

WELL-BEING

This ceremony is carried out at the request of a group of people. When possible, the participants are seated. The Officiant and Assistant are standing.

Assistant: We are gathered here to turn our thoughts to those dear to us. Some of them are facing difficulties in their emotional lives, some in their relationships with others, some with their health. To them we direct our thoughts and our best hopes.

Officiant: We have faith that our call for well-being will reach them. Let us think of those dear to us. Let us feel the presence of those dear to us. Let us experience contact with those dear to us.

Assistant: Let us take some time to meditate on the difficulties that they are facing...

A few minutes are given so that the participants may meditate.

Officiant: Now we would like these people to feel our best hopes for them. A wave of relief and well-being will reach them...

Assistant: Let us take a short time to mentally locate the situation of well-being that we wish for our loved ones...

A few minutes are given for participants to concentrate their minds on this.

Officiant: We conclude this ceremony by allowing the opportunity, for those who desire, to feel the presence of those loved ones who, *although they are not here in our time or in our space,* are connected to us in this experience of love, peace, and warm joy…

A short time is given for this.

Officiant: This has been good for others, comforting for us, and inspiring for our lives… Greetings to everyone immersed in this current of well-being, which has been strengthened by the best wishes of all those present…

PROTECTION

This ceremony may be carried out for an individual or a group. Everyone is standing. The Officiant and the Assistant are facing the children, who are surrounded by the other participants.

Assistant: The purpose of this ceremony is to give children participation in our community.

Since ancient times, children have been the focus of ceremonies such as namings and baptisms. Through these ceremonies people have recognized a change of status, in stage of life.

There are today and have long been civil formalities that record the date and place of birth and other information. However, the spiritual transcendence that accompanies a ceremony of this kind has nothing to do with the cold formalities of written documents. Rather, it flows from the joy of parents, family, and friends when children are publicly introduced to the community.

This is a ceremony through which the status of children changes as they become participants in a community that makes a commitment to be responsible for them should unfortunate events leave them unprotected.

This ceremony requests protection for this child (these children), and the community welcomes them as new sons and daughters.

Following a brief pause, the Officiant addresses those present in a warm tone.

Officiant: We ask protection for this child (these children).

Assistant: We welcome them with joy, and commit ourselves to their protection.

Officiant: We extend our best wishes... Peace and joy for all!

The Officiant gently lays a hand on the head of each child, kissing each one on the forehead.

MARRIAGE

Everyone is standing. For one or more couples. The Officiant and the Assistant face the couple(s).

Assistant: Since ancient times marriage has been a ceremony that marks a change of status for people.

When we end or begin a new stage in life it is often accompanied by a corresponding ritual. Our personal and social lives are marked by rituals that, to a greater or lesser degree, we accept as customary. We greet one another in the morning differently than we do at night; we shake hands upon meeting people; we celebrate birthdays, graduations, and new jobs. Our sporting events are accompanied by rituals, and our religious, political, and civic ceremonies place us in the appropriate attitude for each occasion.

Marriage is an important change in the status of people, and one for which all nations require certain legal formalities. That is, the marital relationship places the spouses in a new situation with respect to the community and the State. However, when a couple establishes the bond of marriage, they do so thinking of a new way of life. They do so with profound feelings and not merely as a formality.

Consequently, in this ceremony that marks a change of status, the partners have the intention to establish a new and hopefully lasting union with one another. They have the desire to receive the best from each other, and to give the best to each other. And they also intend to carry this relationship further by bringing children into the world or adopting them.

Seeing marriage in this way, we may acknowledge the importance of the legal formalities of this union, but in the spiritual and emotional sense we say that only the couple endows this ceremony with meaning. In other words, this ceremony brings two human beings to the situation of undertaking a new life, and through this ceremony the partners establish this profound union in accordance with their own feelings.

We do not marry them; they marry one another before our community.

Officiant: In order for this ceremony to be true and your own, we ask (addressing one partner): What is this marriage for you?

The one addressed by the Officiant responds aloud.

Officiant: *(addressing the other partner):* What is this marriage for you?

The one addressed by the Officiant responds aloud.

Officiant: Then this marriage will be in accordance with your expressed desires and your most profound intentions. *(Greets the couple(s) affectionately).*

ASSISTANCE

This is a ceremony of great affection, requiring the person performing it to give the best of himself or herself.

The ceremony may be repeated at the request of the person receiving it or those caring for him or her.

The Officiant is alone with the dying person.

Regardless of whether person who is dying appears lucid or unconscious, the Officiant comes close to them and speaks slowly in a voice that is soft and clear.

Officiant: The memories of your life are the judgment of your actions. You can, in a short time, recall much of what is best in you. Remember then, but without fear, and purify your memory. Gently remember, and calm your mind...

The Officiant remains silent for a few minutes, and then resumes reading in a voice of the same tone and intensity.

Reject startling fears and disheartenment...

Reject the desire to flee toward low and dark regions...

Reject the attachment to memories...

Remain in internal liberty, indifferent toward the dream of the landscape...

....

Resolve now to begin the ascent...

The pure Light dawns in the summits of the great mountain chains, and the waters-of-a-thou-sand-colors flow amid unrecognizable melodies toward crystalline plateaus and prairies...

Do not fear the pressure of the Light which pushes against you with increasing strength the closer you draw to its center. Absorb it as though it were a liquid or a wind, for certainly, in it is life...

When you find the hidden city in the great mountain chain, you must know the entrance— and you will know it in the moment your life is transformed. Its enormous walls are written in fig-ures, are written in colors, are "sensed." In this city are kept the done and the yet-to-be-done...

The Officiant leaves a brief silence, and then resumes reading in a voice of the same tone and intensity.

Now you are reconciled...

You are purified...

Prepare to enter the most beautiful City of Light, this city never seen by the eye, whose song has never been heard by human ears...

Come, prepare to enter the most beautiful Light...

DEATH

Officiant: Life has ceased in this body. We must now make an effort to separate in our minds the image of this body from the image of the person we remember...

This body does not hear us. This body is not the person we remember...

May those of you who do not feel the presence here of another life, separate from the body, consider that although death has paralyzed this body, the actions he/she carried out will continue to act, and their influence will never end. This chain of actions that was set in motion in life cannot be stopped by death. How profound it is to meditate on this truth, even though we may not completely comprehend the transformation of one action into another!

And may those of you who do feel the presence of a separate life consider that death has only paralyzed this body, that the mind has once again triumphantly freed itself, opening its way toward the Light...

Whatever our views, let us not weep for this body. Rather, let us meditate on the root of our beliefs, and a gentle and silent joy will come to us...

Peace in the heart, light in the understanding!

RECOGNITION

Recognition is a ceremony of inclusion in the Community, inclusion through common experiences, shared ideals, attitudes, and common procedures.

The ceremony is carried out at the request of a group of people and following a Service. Those who will participate should have the written text.

The Officiant and Assistant stand.

Assistant: This ceremony has been requested by people who wish to actively include themselves in our Community. Through this Ceremony they express a personal and social commitment to work to improve their own lives and the lives of those around them.

The Assistant invites those who wish to give testimony to stand.

Officiant: The pain and suffering that human beings experience recedes when good knowledge advances, not knowledge at the service of selfishness and oppression.

Good knowledge leads to justice.

Good knowledge leads to reconciliation.

Good knowledge also leads us to decipher the sacred in the depths of our consciousness.

Assistant *(and those giving testimony read):*

We consider the human being to be the highest value—above money, the State, religion, the models, and social systems.

We promote liberty of thought.

We promote equal rights and equal opportunities for all human beings.

We recognize and applaud diversity in customs and cultures.

We oppose all discrimination.

We consecrate just resistance against all forms of violence: physical, economic, racial, religious, sexual, psychological, and moral.

Officiant: Just as no one has the right to discriminate against others for their religion or their non-religiousness, we affirm our right to proclaim our spirituality and our belief in immortality and the sacred.

Our spirituality is not the spirituality of superstition, it is not the spirituality of intolerance, it is not the spirituality of dogma, it is not the spirituality of religious violence. It is the spirituality that has awakened from its deep sleep to nurture the best aspirations of the human being. *(cont.)*

Assistant *(and those giving testimony read):*

We want to give coherence to our lives, to make coincide what we think, what we feel, and what we do.

We want to surpass bad conscience by acknowledging our failures.

We aspire to persuade and to reconcile.

We make a commitment to increasingly fulfill the rule that reminds us to "treat others as we want to be treated."

Officiant: Let us begin a new life.

Let us search within ourselves for the signs of the sacred, and let us carry our message to others.

Assistant *(and those giving testimony read):*

Today we begin to renew our lives. Let us begin by seeking mental peace and the Force that gives us joy and conviction. Afterwards, let us go to those closest to us and share with them everything great and good that has happened to us.

Officiant: Peace, Force, and Joy for everyone.

Assistant *(and all those present):*

For you also, Peace, Force, and Joy.

THE PATH

If you believe that your life will end with death, nothing that you think, feel, or do has any meaning. Everything will end with incoherence and disintegration.

If you believe that your life does not end with death, you must bring into agreement what you think with what you feel and what you do. All must advance toward coherence, toward unity.

If you are indifferent to the pain and suffering of others, none of the help that you ask for will find justification.

If you are not indifferent to the pain and suffering of others, in order to help them you must bring your thoughts, feelings, and actions into agreement.

Learn to treat others in the way that you want to be treated.

Learn to surpass pain and suffering in yourself, in those close to you, and in human society.

Learn to resist the violence that is within you and outside of you.

Learn to recognize the signs of the sacred within you and around you.

Do not let your life pass by without asking yourself, "Who am I?"

Do not let your life pass by without asking yourself, "Where am I going?"

Do not let a day pass by without giving an answer to yourself about who you are.

Do not let a day pass by without giving an answer to yourself about where you are going.

Do not let a great joy pass without giving thanks internally.

Do not let a great sadness pass without calling into your interior for the joy that you have saved there.

Do not imagine that you are alone in your village, in your city, on the Earth, or among the infinite worlds.

Do not imagine that you are enchained to this time and this space.

Do not imagine that in your death loneliness will become eternal.

For information on Silo's Message see
www.silosmessage.net
www.silo.net

www.ingramcontent.com/pod-product-compliance
Lightning Source LLC
Chambersburg PA
CBHW020513030426
42337CB00011B/368